20th Century

Sport

Andrew Langley

Titles in this series

**Art
Cinema
Communications
Farming
Fashion
Industry
Medicine
Music
Science
Sport
Transport
Warfare**

**Series Editor: William Wharfe
Designer: Ross George**

Front cover *Windsurfing is one of the latest twentieth century sports. Expert windsurfer Jenna de Rosnay leaps into the air with her sailboard.*
Back cover *Jessie Owens hurtles away to win the 200 m at the Berlin Olympics in 1936.*
Frontispiece *Erwin Resch of Austria 'in flight' during the downhill skiing competition at Wengen, Switzerland, in 1989.*

First published in 1989 by
Wayland (Publishers) Ltd
61 Western Road, Hove
East Sussex BN3 1JD, England

© Copyright 1989 Wayland (Publishers) Ltd

British Library Cataloguing in Publication Data
Langley, Andrew
Twentieth century sport.
1. Sports – For children
I. Title II. Series
796

ISBN 1–85210–625–5

Typeset by L. George & R. Gibbs, Wayland
Printed by G. Canale and C.S.p.A, Turin, Italy
Bound by Casterman, S.A, Belgium

Contents

1900 – 1914 The Golden Age

Making the rules	4
The changing face of sport	6
For love and money	7
Exporting sport	8
The first black champions	9

1918 – 1932 New Heroes

Individual sports	10
The first World Cup	11
The record-breakers	12
Women stars	14

1932 – 1950 Troubled Times

The bodyline affair	16
Money talks	18
The shadow of war	20

1950 – 1968 New Horizons

The old order changes	22
The records tumble	24
The end of the amateur	26
Sport and television	28

1968 – 1982 International Problems

Out in the cold	30
The unhappy Games	32
The media and sport	34
On the way up	36

1982 – 1990 Into the 1990s

Read that label!	38
Violence on and off the field	40
Wind and wave	42
Mass participation	44

Glossary — 46

Further Reading — 47

Index — 48

The Golden Age

Before 1900, few countries of the world had well-organized sports, and even fewer played matches against each other. All this was to change rapidly at the turn of the century, largely due to the improvements taking place in international transport.

Making the rules

Right W.G. Grace was the most famous cricketer of the Victorian age.

Below Lord's Cricket Ground in London has always been the headquarters of English cricket. This is how it looked in 1874.

Towards the end of the nineteenth century, most games were well-established. A form of football had been played in Ancient China, and hockey in Ancient Greece. Cricket had been known in Britain for over six hundred years. Tennis had also been developed in the Middle Ages. But around 1900, there came a great increase in the popularity of these and other sports. For the first time, games were strictly organized, and the rules of play were written down. Many new sporting events were started, and teams travelled long distances to compete with each other.

Among the first sports to become established was cricket. By 1900, test matches were being played regularly between

England, Australia and South Africa. This was the Golden Age of cricket when huge crowds gathered to watch W.G. Grace, Victor Trumper, Archie Maclaren and other great players.

Tennis was also a firm favourite. There were national championships in Britain, the USA, Australia and New Zealand. The Davis Cup competition was founded in 1900 and within a few years nine nations were competing. In the USA, team sports were developing rapidly. American football, based on rugby football, was fast growing in popularity, and baseball's first World Series was played in 1903. The team sports of basketball, netball and volleyball were all invented in the USA in the 1890s.

One of the most important sporting events was the Olympic Games, founded in Ancient Greece. They were revived in 1896 after a gap of 1,500 years. The early meetings were not well organized and few nations took part. By 1908, however, they had become the most important event in the sporting calendar, with twenty-one different competitions.

Above It looks as if Dorando of Italy has won the 1908 Olympic Marathon in London. But judges later disqualified him because he was helped over the line. He was given a consolation medal instead.

Left Jim Thorpe of the USA winning the discus during the pentathlon at the 1912 Olympics.

Above A lawn tennis party in the early 1900s. The women players wore long skirts and straw hats.

The changing face of sport

Ninety years ago, the clothing and equipment of games players looked very different. British footballers wore long, tight-fitting trousers and heavy boots with leather studs fixed to the soles. The ball was not waterproof and became very heavy in wet weather. At first, American footballers wore little protective clothing, but the game soon proved to be very dangerous. In 1905 alone, eighteen college players were killed while playing the sport.

Soon afterwards players began wearing shoulder pads and simple leather helmets. Cricketers also needed protection. In those days none wore helmets and only a few players wore gloves. Their only guard against the hard leather ball was a pair of leg-pads and the bat itself.

It is hard to imagine how women of the 1900s could play tennis wearing big straw hats and long, full skirts. Some wore ties as well!

For love and money

The idea of being paid for sporting activities was still quite new in 1900. Athletes and tennis players were all amateurs and could not take payment for performing in tournaments. On the other hand, many footballers and cricketers were paid professionals, but their earnings were extremely small.

Golf was fast becoming popular, especially in Scotland. The golf clubs employed professional players to coach their members. Though they were poorly paid, the professionals were able to add to their earnings by selling, and even making golfing equipment.

Betting had played an important part in horse-racing for many years. Bookmakers made fortunes by taking bets from the spectators. The racehorse owners often won large sums in prize money. In contrast, the jockeys themselves were usually paid very little.

Left *Horse-racing is known as 'the sport of kings'. Here, King Edward VII (centre, top) watches a race at Epsom in 1902.*

Exporting sport

During this period, travel became easier and faster. When people went to other countries for holidays or to work, they took their national sports with them. Football, which had been founded in England, was established in Europe by British visitors. The England team played its first overseas match in 1908, against Austria. Soon after this, Europeans took football to South America, where it quickly became very popular. Brazil formed a Football Association in 1914, soon to be followed by Uruguay and Argentina.

The European sports of tennis and golf were soon adopted in North America, and professionals went to the USA to give coaching lessons and help to set up clubs. At about the same time, Americans were helping to promote the new sport of basketball in Europe and the Far East. Cricket, too, was spreading to many of the countries that were then part of the British Empire, including Australia, New Zealand, South Africa, India and the West Indies.

Above The Corinthians football team at the Crystal Palace ground in 1905. It was men like these who took the game to Europe and South America.

Right Basketball was first played in the USA in 1891. Here is one of the pioneer high school teams from Newport, Rhode Island.

The first black champions

In December 1908, there was a fight for the heavyweight boxing championship of the world between Tommy Burns of Canada and Jack Johnson of the USA. Johnson won it easily. He was tall, lithe and a brilliant boxer. He was in fact the first black man to become a major sports star and went on to be one of the finest heavyweight boxers of all time.

At every fight, the white spectators jeered at him, and when Johnson defeated another white favourite, Jim Jeffries, there were race riots in the southern USA. At this time it was difficult for black sportsmen to break through the barriers of racial prejudice. Almost all of the national competitions were restricted to white contestants only during these years.

Above *Amid the jeers of the crowd, Jack Johnson knocks out the white hero Jim Jeffries in 1910.*

1918-1932

New Heroes

During the First World War, hardly any sport was played in Europe. International sport came to a standstill. At the end of the war, people were hungry for entertainment. They found it on the sports fields, where they could watch a new generation of glamorous, record-breaking stars.

Individual sports

In the 1920s, the individual sports, in which the players competed on their own, became more and more popular and the leading personalities became world news. At this time American golfers such as Walter Hagen and Bobby Jones were the best in the world. In tennis, too, American players were the most successful. Players like 'Big Bill' Tilden and Helen Wills won championships in England, France and the USA. However, the competition was strong and included the French tennis star, Suzanne Lenglen. Between 1919 and 1926, she won the women's singles six times at Wimbledon, and in 1926 she turned professional.

At the Olympic Games of 1924 and 1928, American athletes took most of the medals. Skating and skiing were popular winter sports after the end of the First World War, and in 1924 the first Winter Olympic Games were held at Chamonix in France.

Right *A game of ice hockey in progress in the 1930s. The sport was first developed in Canada in the 1850s, but only became widely popular in the 1920s.*

The first World Cup

Association football, or soccer, quickly became the most popular game in the world. Clubs flourished in Western and Eastern Europe, and in South America. The sport followed the rules laid down by the Federation of International Football Associations (FIFA). In 1929, FIFA put forward an exciting idea. They would organize a competition between the footballing nations. It was to be known as the World Cup, and the winner would receive a gold trophy presented by the president, Jules Rimet, a French lawyer after whom the cup was named.

It came as something of a surprise when Uruguay was chosen as the host nation for the first World Cup finals in 1930. But there were two good reasons. The Uruguayans were the Olympic football champions at the time, and they were also celebrating the centenary of their independence. Although only thirteen countries competed, the finals were extremely successful and the Uruguayan team won.

Above *The very first football World Cup is presented to the President of the Uruguayan Football Association in 1930.*

The record-breakers

Few periods have witnessed so many sporting giants as the late 1920s and the early 1930s. They thrilled the spectators and set up astonishing new records. Many of these great achievements have never been bettered.

'Big Bill' Tilden ruled the men's tennis circuit in the 1920s. Between 1920 and 1927 he did not lose a single important match. Tilden won the American championships seven times, and was Wimbledon champion three times.

Johnny Weissmuller is well known today for his film role as Tarzan, but he was also one of the greatest swimmers of all time. He won five Olympic gold medals in 1924 and 1928, and his record for the 100 m freestyle swimming event was unbeaten for seventeen years.

Paavo Nurmi of Finland established twenty-two world records in athletics. At the 1924 Olympics he won all four of his races. He ran two of them, the 1,500 m and 5,000 m races, within ninety minutes of each other.

Right The American golfer Bobby Jones was the first player to do the Grand Slam. He won the open and amateur championships in both Britain and the USA in 1930.

Below Johnny Weissmuller poses in his film role as Tarzan. He was also one of the greatest of all swimming champions.

Right Jack Dempsey reigned as world heavyweight boxing champion between 1919 and 1926.

Right Left-handed 'Babe' Ruth set many records in his career from 1914 to 1935.

George 'Babe' Ruth was the great hero of American baseball. In the 1927 season he hit 60 home runs, a record that stood for over thirty years. In his career he hit 714 home runs.

In 1928, Dixie Dean of Everton set a football record that may never be beaten. During the English season he scored 82 goals, including 60 in league games. In his whole career he scored an outstanding total of 451 goals.

For eight years the American Bobby Jones dominated the golfing world. In that time he won thirteen major titles, and capped his career in 1930 by becoming open and amateur champion of both Britain and the USA.

Don Bradman of Australia was the greatest run scorer that cricket has ever seen. In five test matches against England in 1930, he totalled 974 runs, more than anyone else before or since. In a single day's play at Leeds, he scored 309 runs, also a record.

Women stars

In 1919 a young French tennis player came to Wimbledon for the first time. In her first four matches she lost only six games. She went on to become singles champion at the age of nineteen. Her name was Suzanne Lenglen. Before her arrival, nobody had taken women's tennis very seriously, but Lenglen soon turned it into a great spectacle. She was an exciting and energetic performer on the court. She wore shorter skirts than any of the other women players, finding that the more traditional long skirts inhibited her play.

Suzanne Lenglen built up an astounding record. She won fifteen titles at Wimbledon, eighteen in France and two in the Olympics of 1920. She was succeeded as queen of the tennis court by the American Helen Wills Moody. Icy and unexcitable, Moody dominated women's tennis between 1927 and 1935.

At last, female players and athletes were beginning to draw the crowds and appear in the headlines. In 1926 Gertrude Ederle became the first woman to swim the

Above Helen Wills Moody was all but unbeatable on the tennis court in the 1930s. She did not lose a set at Wimbledon over seven years.

Right Gertrude Ederle is given a final coat of grease before setting out to swim the English Channel in 1926.

Left Sonja Henie was the women's world ice-skating champion between 1927 and 1936. She later became a film star.

Far left Mildred 'Babe' Didrikson won two gold medals at the 1932 Olympics. Then she took up golf, and became US Open champion three times.

English Channel, taking fourteen hours to do so – two hours faster than the existing record, which was held by a man.

In the 1928 Olympic Games in Amsterdam, women's athletic events were included for the first time. Very few nations sent women's teams and the spectators paid little attention. It was a different story at the Los Angeles Olympics in 1932. A Texan teenager named 'Babe' Didrikson won the javelin, the 80 m hurdles and the high jump to become the first Olympic heroine. She was only allowed a silver medal for the high jump because the judges did not like her 'head first' jumping action. Later, she took up golf, achieving international fame by winning championships, and by driving the ball immense distances despite her small size.

The Norwegian Sonja Henie was one of the greatest of all figure-skaters. World champion and unbeaten between 1927 and 1936, she won gold medals at three consecutive Olympics. On retiring from the ice rink, she became a successful film star.

Troubled Times

By the 1930s, international sport played an important part in everyday life. Though most people just wanted to watch their favourite sport, there were others who saw it as a source of wealth. As war drew near, sport fell victim to the whims and wishes of the new leaders.

The bodyline affair

Below *Don Bradman on his way to a century (100 runs) at a test match in Nottingham, England. Bodyline bowling was developed to try and curb his high scoring.*

In the autumn of 1932, an England cricket team landed in Australia. The captain, Douglas Jardine, was determined to win the test series. He had a special plan to prevent Australia's best batsman, Don Bradman, from making his usual high scores. The idea came to be known as 'bodyline bowling'. England's fastest bowlers, Harold Larwood and Bill Voce, were to aim the ball at the leg stump or outside. Such bowling was difficult and dangerous to face.

The first two test matches were tense and evenly fought, but in the third match the trouble started. A ball from Larwood hit the Australian captain over the heart. He collapsed but continued his innings. Soon the crowd was booing. There was an

Above Australian batsman Bert Oldfield is hit on the head by a ball from Harold Larwood.

Above Harold Larwood, the English bowler at the centre of the 'bodyline' issue.

even greater uproar next day when another batsman was injured by Larwood.

The Australian cricket board sent a telegram to the MCC in London, calling Jardine's bodyline strategy unsportsmanlike. The MCC tried hard to calm things down. The tour carried on, and England won, but sport had come near to causing a rift between two friendly nations.

There were several unpleasant sporting events in the years before the Second World War. Most of these occurred in matches between nations that were far from friendly with each other. One of the worst was the football international between England and Italy in 1934. Italy was at that time a Fascist country under the leadership of Mussolini, and wanted to win at all costs. The Italian players used their boots and fists to attack their opponents, but still lost the match.

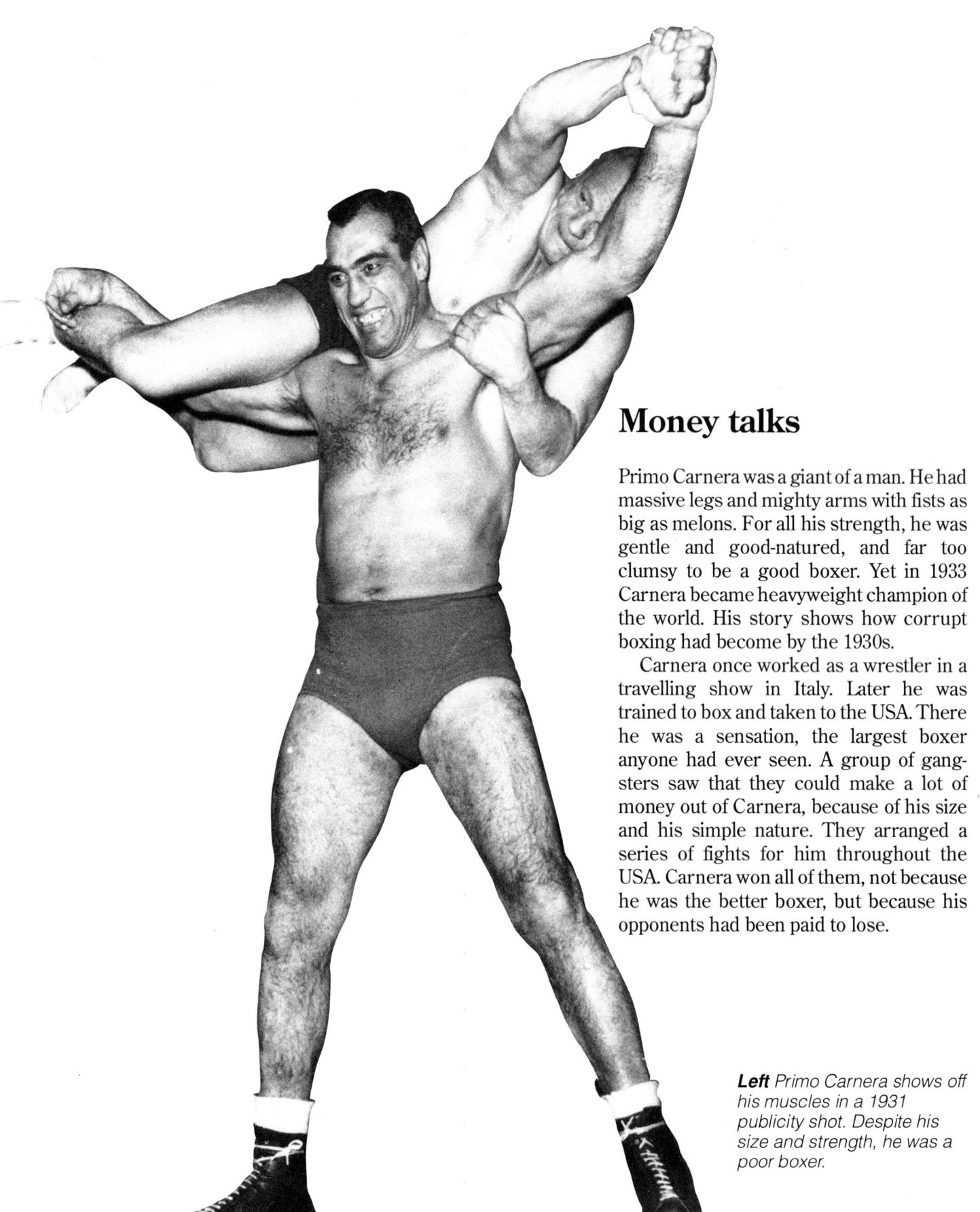

Money talks

Primo Carnera was a giant of a man. He had massive legs and mighty arms with fists as big as melons. For all his strength, he was gentle and good-natured, and far too clumsy to be a good boxer. Yet in 1933 Carnera became heavyweight champion of the world. His story shows how corrupt boxing had become by the 1930s.

Carnera once worked as a wrestler in a travelling show in Italy. Later he was trained to box and taken to the USA. There he was a sensation, the largest boxer anyone had ever seen. A group of gangsters saw that they could make a lot of money out of Carnera, because of his size and his simple nature. They arranged a series of fights for him throughout the USA. Carnera won all of them, not because he was the better boxer, but because his opponents had been paid to lose.

Left Primo Carnera shows off his muscles in a 1931 publicity shot. Despite his size and strength, he was a poor boxer.

Eventually, in 1934, Carnera beat Jack Sharkey to become world heavyweight champion. This fight, too, was almost certainly 'fixed'. His reign did not last long. A year later he was battered to defeat by a boxer who could not be bribed to lose and his brief career was at an end. His gangster managers had taken all his prize money and Primo Carnera returned to Italy without a penny.

This form of corruption was not unusual in the boxing world and also occurred in horse-racing and greyhound racing from time to time. Sometimes horses were doped with cocaine to make them run faster and win. Likely winners were deliberately lamed, or had their nostrils blocked to make them run more slowly and lose. Jockeys were even threatened or bribed to lose races. Such malpractices are now carefully watched out for by sporting organizations like the Jockey Club.

Left In one of his last fights, Carnera was beaten by Joe Louis. Louis went on to become one of the finest of all heavyweight champions.

Below During the 1930s the German government poured huge sums of money into the development of racing cars. Here Muller leads the field in 1938 in a German Auto-Union racer.

The shadow of war

In 1936 Europe was drifting towards war. Germany was led by Adolf Hitler and his Nazi party, who were building up strong armed forces and bullying their weaker neighbours. By a strange twist of fate, the Olympic Games were held that year in Berlin, the German capital.

Foreign athletes arrived in Berlin to find that the Games had been designed to glorify Hitler rather than sport. Swastika flags dominated the stadium. In a grand opening ceremony the crowds cheered and saluted

Top right *The poster advertising the 1936 Olympic Games in Berlin.*

Bottom right *Adolf Hitler gives the Nazi salute at the opening ceremony of the Berlin Olympics. He is dressed in military uniform.*

their leader. There were Nazi troops to be seen everywhere.

Hitler strongly believed that the white Germans ('Aryans') were superior to any other race, particularly Jewish and black people. He hoped that the Olympic Games would prove this. When the German football team was beaten, he was so angry that he sent them home in disgrace. Hitler was even more enraged by the success of a black American – Jesse Owens. This brilliant athlete won gold medals in the 100 metres, 200 metres, long jump and 100 metres relay, easily defeating his white and 'Aryan' rivals. Hitler, who had congratulated several other winners, refused to shake the hand of Jesse Owens.

In Berlin, Hitler had used sport as a weapon in his fight for political power. This unhappy mixture of sport and politics became more evident as the Second World War approached. Hitler seized control of Austria in 1938, after which Austrian players were forced to wear German colours. In that same year, England played Germany at football in Berlin. The English players, much against their will, were ordered to give the Nazi salute before the game. The British government had hoped that this would please the German leader. However, the England team soon displeased him greatly by defeating their opponents by six goals to three.

Left A gold medal for Jesse Owens at the Berlin Olympics. He wins the long jump with a record leap.

Bottom left Jesse Owens takes off at the start of the 100 metres at Berlin.

1950-1968

New Horizons

Until the Second World War, sport had been dominated by the large and developed nations of the world. But during the 1950s many smaller and developing nations began to produce their own teams and stars. This was to make sport even more widely international.

The old order changes

In 1950 the England cricket team had a shock. It was beaten at home for the very first time by the West Indies. West Indian cricket had been growing stronger since the end of the war, but now it had produced one of the finest sides ever seen. Besides the brilliant batting of Walcott, Weekes and Worrell, the team included two devastating slow bowlers, Ramadhin and Valentine.

During the 1950s, New Zealand, with a population of only 2 million, fielded the strongest Rugby Union side in the world. Between 1953 and 1967, the New Zealanders toured Britain three times. In those years they won sixty-three of their matches and lost only three.

There were shocks for Britain on the soccer pitch as well. England, who had taught the world to play football, had never been beaten at home. But in 1953 they met a superb Hungarian team who beat them at Wembley by six goals to three. A few

Right *The 18 year old Pelé of Brazil attacks during the 1958 World Cup. Brazil won the competition for the first time.*

months later the Hungarians won again, this time by seven goals to one.

By 1958, however, the kings of world soccer were South American. Brazil, with stars such as Garrincha and Pelé, won the World Cup, a feat they repeated in 1962. When Brazil won for a record third time in 1970, they were given the trophy to keep. Teams now compete for a new World Cup.

There were new sporting heroes from Africa. In 1960 an Ethiopian named Abebe Bikila surprised the world by winning the Olympic marathon and so becoming the first African to win a gold medal. Bikila won the marathon again in 1964. Four years later, more African runners appeared on the Olympic scene. Three Kenyans, Keino, Biwott and Temu, won golds in the long distance races, as did Gammoudi of Tunisia. Black Africa had brought a new excitement to athletics.

Above This era saw new standards of skill and professionalism in American football. This shot shows Andy Nelson of the Baltimore Colts fly-tackling Tom Wilson of the Los Angeles Rams (left) in a game in 1960. The Rams won 10–3.

Left Abebe Bikila of Ethiopia became the first black African gold medallist when he won the Olympic marathon in Rome in 1960.

The records tumble

The 1950s and the 1960s were years of outstanding achievements in sport and athletics. Not only were many new records set, but barriers like the four-minute mile were broken for the first time. Here is a calendar of some of those memorable events and achievements.

1951 'Sugar' Ray Robinson became world middleweight boxing champion for the first time in his career. He was to lose the title and win it back four more times.

1954 Roger Bannister set the record for running a mile in under four minutes. John Landy broke it six weeks later.

1955 Donald Campbell set a new water-speed record of 202 mph. In 1964 he also broke the land-speed record in his famous car, *Bluebird*.

1956 Jim Laker took 19 wickets out of a possible 20 in a cricket test match against Australia. This record has never since been beaten.

1958 Gary Sobers scored 365 runs not out for the West Indies in a cricket test match against Pakistan, the highest test match innings ever.

Top right Al Oerter on his way to winning the 1956 Olympic discus gold medal. He achieved gold at this event in the following three Olympics. Each time he had to fight hard to win.

Right A tragic end to a great career. Donald Campbell's speedboat Bluebird overturns in 1967 and he is killed instantly.

Left West Indian Gary Sobers was the greatest all-rounder cricket has ever seen. He was a brilliant batsman and fielder, and could bowl in three different styles.

Below Surrounded by small boats, Francis Chichester in Gipsy Moth IV sails into Plymouth in 1967. He had sailed around the world in 226 days.

1961 Roger Maris of the New York Yankees broke 'Babe' Ruth's long-standing baseball record by hitting 61 home runs in one season.
1966 Jim Brown retired from American football. In his nine-year career he gained a total of 12,312 yards and made a record 126 touchdowns.
1967 Francis Chichester sailed solo around the world in only 226 days in his yacht *Gipsy Moth IV*. He returned in May and was knighted by Queen Elizabeth later that year.
1968 American Al Oerter won the discus gold medal at the Mexico Olympics, the fourth successive Games at which he achieved this. This is perhaps the most remarkable of all Olympic records ever achieved.

Above *Muhammad Ali meets Britain's Henry Cooper before a title fight in 1966. Ali won the world heavyweight boxing championship a record three times.*

The end of the amateur

By the late 1960s there were very few amateur, unpaid players left in sport. Almost all top-class sportsmen and sportswomen were receiving payment to perform in public, and some were earning very large sums of money.

The richest prize in all sport was the heavyweight boxing title. In 1962 Sonny Liston became the new world champion, winning a fight in less than three minutes. For this he was paid $282,000. Nine years later, when the great Muhammad Ali fought Joe Frazier, the two boxers shared over $5 million between them.

Ever since they began, the major lawn tennis competitions had been for amateur players only. The professionals, who were often the best players, could only play against each other in exhibition matches. Then, in 1968, professionals were allowed to compete in the Paris and Wimbledon championships. Soon, top players like Margaret Court and Rod Laver were earning over $100,000 a year.

Tennis players could now afford to take part in international events throughout the world. The same applied for motor-racing drivers and also for golfers. Arnold Palmer, for instance, made so much money during the 1960s that he quickly became a millionaire. Amateurs did not last long in cricket, either. For more than a century they had played alongside paid professionals, but in 1963 the distinction between the two was abolished. Within a few years there were no amateurs playing in first-class cricket.

A few sports, however, maintained their amateur status. No one was allowed to play Rugby Union if he had accepted payment for any kind of sport. Only amateurs were permitted to take part in the Olympic Games and other major athletic competitions.

Right Rod Laver, Australian professional tennis player. He took part in the first 'open' Wimbledon championship in 1968.

Below Arnold Palmer was the first golfer to become a millionaire. In 1962 and 1963, he won more than $200,000 in prize money.

Sport and television

The first major sporting event to be televised was the Olympic Games of 1936 in Berlin. The pictures could only be received in Germany. Since few Germans owned television sets, people crowded into local halls and theatres to watch.

A year later, viewers in England were able to watch Rugby Union from Twickenham and tennis from Wimbledon. Shortly after that, test match cricket was seen for the first time on the screen. During the 1950s, television reception improved greatly, and millions of people throughout the world began to watch a variety of sports regularly without leaving their homes.

The audience for sporting occasions thus grew to be enormous. At first, live coverage of events was limited. But Australian audiences, for instance, were able to see highlights of cricket test matches taking place in England only a few hours after they had been recorded on camera. Worldwide interest in events such as the cycling Tour de France and Grand Prix motor-racing made these sports more popular.

Most important and popular of all were the Olympic Games. In 1960 the Games were held in Rome. For the first time television pictures were relayed live to neighbouring countries.

Right *The Tour de France, 1961. The riders have reached the thirteenth stage of the gruelling 4,000 km race.*

Left Rugby Union became a popular sport in England in the 1950s and 1960s through television. Here the South African Springboks team play Cardiff in 1960.

Below Grand Prix racing at Silverstone in 1967.

Four years later, the Tokyo Olympics were relayed by satellite all over the world. These Games were watched by over 500 million viewers each day.

Television companies paid huge fees for the right to televise such events. In the USA, sport could be seen at all hours of the day and night. Eventually, a new television channel appeared, showing nothing but sport, most of it recorded. By far the most popular game was American football. During any weekend in the season, fans could watch non-stop live football for more than twenty-four hours.

International Problems

During the 1970s, sport attracted more spectators and more money than ever before. Yet there were occasions when sport was upset by international problems. At this time televised sport became more commercial and the big stars began to expect larger rewards for their efforts.

Out in the cold

Since 1948, South Africa has lived with a system called apartheid, in which white people are treated differently from non-white people. Many nations of the world disapproved of apartheid and urged the South African government to abolish it. Before long, sport was mixed up in the apartheid problem.

The South African team at the 1960 Olympic Games contained no black athletes. Many other teams, notably the USSR and other African nations, protested at this. The result was that South Africa was not invited to compete in the next Games.

Below Anti-apartheid demonstrators protest against the presence of South African rugby players in a match in London.

Top left In 1982 a party of rebel English cricketers toured South Africa. As a result they were banned from test cricket for three years.

Bottom left South African Zola Budd became a British citizen so that she could take part in international athletics competitions. However, due largely to pressure from anti-apartheid demonstrators, she eventually returned to South Africa.

South Africa has not taken part since. But this was only the beginning of the country's exclusion from world sport. In 1968 the South African tennis team was expelled from the Davis Cup.

Soon afterwards, England selected a cricket team to tour South Africa. It included Basil d'Oliveira, a non-white player who had been born in Cape Town. The South African government refused to accept a team with a non-white sportsman in it. England would not change the team and the tour was cancelled. Within a few years, South Africa had been barred from international cricket altogether.

Rugby Union, one of South Africa's most popular sports, suffered as well. In 1969 a tour to England was cancelled, and the last visit by a British Lions side took place in 1980. South Africa's rugby authorities have tried to make the game more open to all races. In 1981 their national team included a black player, Errol Tobias, for the first time. But the system of apartheid continued and South Africa remained isolated from the rest of the sporting world.

The unhappy Games

The Olympic Games are the most famous sporting event in the world. Hundreds of athletes from many nations gather to take part. Millions throughout the world watch the competitions on television. But this enormous popularity has brought with it a number of problems. It is sad, but not surprising, that the Olympic movement with its international aims has often been beset by difficulties.

There have been a number of problems in recent times. In 1968, the Olympics were due to take place in Mexico City. Mexico was a poor country, yet huge sums of money were spent on building a new stadium and sports hall.

Right American Tommie Smith and team-mate John Carlos give the Black Power salute after winning medals in the 200 metres at the 1968 Olympics in Mexico.

Many Mexican students believed that this was an unnecessary waste of money and held several demonstrations. At one of these, over 260 people were killed. There was a further embarrassment during the Games. The American team won the 400 m relay race. As the four black athletes received their gold medals, they raised their fists in the air. This salute was a sign that they supported the Black Power movement in the USA. It was a political gesture and had nothing to do with sport.

The next Games, in Munich in 1972, were spoiled by a dreadful tragedy. In the middle of the contests, a group of Palestinian terrorists calling themselves 'Black September,' stormed the quarters of the Israeli team. Twelve Israelis and five terrorists were killed. A memorial ceremony was held in the Olympic stadium.

After this, the Olympic movement seemed on the point of disintegrating. In 1976, at Montreal, twenty-two African nations stayed away from the Games. They were angry that some countries were still playing sport with South Africa. In 1980, the USA stayed away from the Moscow Olympics as a protest against the USSR for invading Afghanistan. Four years later the USSR and their allies, the Eastern bloc and other nations, responded by not attending the Games in Los Angeles.

Above The bodies of the Israeli hostages are flown home after the tragic events at the 1972 Games in Munich.

Above Jack Nicklaus is the most successful golfer of all time. Over a quarter of a century he won over 70 titles and $5 million in prize money.

The media and sport

Star players in many sports grew rich during the 1970s. Jack Nicklaus, the most successful golfer of all time, became a multi-millionaire. So, too, did the tennis star Martina Navratilova. The boxer Muhammad Ali earned $4,500,000 for a single fight in 1975. Between 1960 and 1981, this great boxer is believed to have earned a fortune of $69 million in 61 fights. Great footballers such as Pelé were paid enormous fees for playing in matches, and Barcelona paid a transfer fee of £5 million for the Argentinian player Diego Maradona in 1982.

In cricket, it was a very different story. Most players were paid a modest wage during the season and for the rest of the year they had to find work as best they could. Even test players were unhappy that their rewards from the game were so

low in comparison with the fees paid to other sportsmen.

But this began to change in 1977. Kerry Packer was an Australian businessman who owned a television channel. He wanted it to be the only channel showing cricket in Australia. When he failed to get his way, he decided to organize his own cricket competition. He offered very large payments to the most famous test players from all over the world if they would agree to play in his World Series cricket contest. Most of the West Indian and Australian teams joined him along with important players from England, Pakistan and South Africa.

The cricket world was split in half. During the winter of 1978, there were two Australian teams. One played against England in traditional test matches, while the other played for Packer's World Series, also known as Packer's Circus. In the end Kerry Packer won the argument. He was allowed to televise most of the cricket in Australia. In return, the Australian authorities received the finance they needed. Test players were glad to be earning more money as well, but the game of cricket would never be quite the same again.

Top left *Professional American basketball players are among the highest paid athletes in the world. Here we see the Los Angeles Lakers (yellow) on the attack against the Philadelphia 76ers.*

Left *Kerry Packer (left) and former England cricket captain Tony Greig. Tony Greig left English cricket to play in Kerry Packer's World Series.*

Right The action in baseball is well-suited to television coverage.

On the way up

Billiards, snooker and darts in their modern form are about a century old. But they have only become really popular as spectator sports in the last twenty years. The reason for this is, of course, television, which has brought these sports a huge new audience. Stars like Steve Davis, Alex 'Hurricane' Higgins (snooker) and Jocky Wilson (darts) have become household names in Britain.

Several other sports have been given a boost in popularity as a direct result of television. Motor-racing won millions of new fans during the 1970s. As a result, new Grand Prix races were organized in Brazil, Hungary, Japan, San Marino and the USA. British sporting enthusiasts, despite their dedication to soccer, soon became fans of

Right Snooker became a hugely popular sport during the 1980s, largely because of television coverage.

Above Soviet gymnast Olga Korbut captivated the crowds at the 1972 Olympics. She won two gold medals.

American football fans when the game was televised in Britain.

Gymnastics came into the headlines during the Olympic Games of 1972. Viewers all over the world were enchanted by the performances of the tiny Soviet gymnast Olga Korbut. When she fell during the bar exercises, she seemed to have lost her chance of a medal. But she came back to win gold medals on the beam and in the floor exercises. Her courage inspired millions of children to take up gymnastics themselves.

Many people also began playing squash and badminton for the first time, thanks to television. During this period the first World Open Championships were held and became regular events. The outstanding squash player of the time was Heather McKay, who was unbeaten in women's matches from 1962 to 1980.

The 1970s also saw the beginning of one of the toughest of all new sports – the triathlon. The first competition called the 'Hawaii Ironman', was held in 1978. The contestants first had to swim 3.8 km, then cycle 180 km and finally run a marathon of 42 km. Triathlon contests began in Europe and the USA in 1982.

Above The success of Robin Cousins at the 1980 Olympics inspired thousands of young skaters.

Into the 1990s

Top sports players became more wealthy and more famous during the 1980s. Most of this money and fame has come from sponsors and from television appearances. While spectator sports continue to attract the crowds, there is now an upsurge in the development of sporting activities in which the individual can take part.

Read that label!

When players take part in spectator sports today, they are likely to be carrying advertisements on their clothing or sporting equipment. Whole teams may advertise a product, such as a make of car or a brand of food product. Sometimes they carry the name of a bank or insurance company. Each time the television camera zooms in on a player, the sponsor's name can be read by thousands, or even millions of viewers.

This is how sponsorship works. A company gives a sum of money to a sports club or individual player. In return, the club or player advertises the name of the sponsor. Star tennis players wear sponsored shoes

Below Today, professional footballers in many countries wear shirts printed with the name of their sponsors.

Above World champion racing driver Alain Prost leads the field in a Grand Prix race. His car carries the names of a tobacco company and an oil company.

and play with sponsored rackets. Grand Prix drivers race in cars that are sponsored for the season, and the name of the sponsor is clearly visible on the driver's overalls and on the car itself. In show jumping, a horse may be named after the sponsor, like Harvey Smith's horse Sanyo Technology.

Sponsors may also provide cash to fund an entire tournament or series. Golf's Ryder Cup is a contest between American and British teams (since 1979 the British have been joined by European players). Today it is sponsored by a whisky firm and is called the Johnnie Walker Ryder Cup. Sponsors such as these give valuable support to sport. Without them, prize money would not be so large and players would not be so well paid. However, sponsorship is a form of advertising, and some sponsors are the makers of cigarettes or alcoholic drinks. There are those that believe that healthy sports and sporting personalities should not be advertising such unhealthy products.

The idea of sponsorship has been adopted by small organizations and schools in order to raise funds for charities. Sponsored walks and marathons provide a means of raising money and are also fun for those taking part.

Above The Washington Redskins meet the Denver Broncos in American football's 1988 Super Bowl. American football is one of the most dangerous of all sports, and so the players wear protective clothing.

Violence on and off the field

There is nothing new about violence in sport. Eight hundred years ago the Mayans of Central America played a very rough kind of ball game. The losing team was often killed as a sacrifice to the gods! There is still violence today amongst the players and their fans.

Some sports are dangerous and violent by their nature. Boxing and wrestling are the most obvious of these. American football can be even more dangerous. Here the job of the linebacker is to hit an opponent with his body as hard as possible. Sometimes two linebackers will hit the same man at once. It is hardly surprising that serious injuries are common in this game.

Every sport is based on a set of rules, including rules to prevent violence. The job of the umpire or the referee is to make sure that these rules are obeyed. But umpires cannot see everything and will sometimes make mistakes. It is up to the players themselves to stick to the rules. If they break the rules of play then the game is spoiled and the result may be an unfair one.

Violent incidents on the field and unfair play set a bad example to the fans who are watching. In Panama, one soccer fan was so angered at the scoring of a goal that he ran onto the pitch, drew a gun and shot the ball! At many football matches, rival gangs have been known to have pitched battles inside the grounds and outside. The most tragic example of this type of violence occurred at the Heysel Stadium in Brussels in 1985. English football supporters began fighting with their rivals and in the riot that followed part of the stadium collapsed. Many fans were killed and the world was deeply shocked.

Above Rival fans fight it out during the 1985 European Cup Final in Brussels. Many fans were killed during the rioting.

Left A brawl breaks out during an ice hockey match between the USA and the USSR in 1988.

Wind and wave

There are two individual sports that have been growing in popularity in recent years for those who like an element of danger. These are hang-gliding and windsurfing. Gliding and sailing require essential, expensive equipment and trailers, but hang-gliding and windsurfing are much less demanding. The equipment is not very expensive and can be packed easily onto the roof of a car.

The modern hang-glider can be stowed in a tubular bag and assembled quickly by the owner at the site where the sport is going to take place. It can be launched, flown and landed by means of the energy in the pilot's legs. The basic design was established in the late 1940s by an American scientist, Dr Francis Rogallo. Started as an experiment by a few enthusiasts, hang-gliding has now become a world sport and there are associations in most countries of the world.

Right Water-skiing is becoming an increasingly popular sport, with professionals competing in events around the world – like this one in the USA.

Below A hang-glider sails on the wind. The most skilful flyers can reach heights of more than 4,000 m and distances of over 300 km.

Windsurfing, or boardsailing, has, in a very short time, achieved world-wide popularity. It was developed in the late 1960s by a Californian engineer, Jim Drake. Windsurfing rapidly became popular in the USA and soon the sport became established in Europe and throughout the world. The price of the equipment is comparable with that of cycling or skiing. All that is required for the sport is an open stretch of water and a light breeze.

The sport was introduced into the Olympic Games in 1984 and the winner was Stephen van den Berg of the Netherlands. There have been some very remarkable speed and endurance achievements by windsurfers. Some have recorded speeds of about 60 kph, and the English Channel was crossed in slightly over one hour by a Frenchman Arnaud de Rosnay.

These two new sports are likely to become even more popular in the 1990s.

Left Windsurfing is an exciting new sport which has grown very popular during the 1980s.

Opposite *Runners cross over the East River by the thousand during the 1989 New York marathon. There are now annual marathons in many major cities.*

Inset *In recent years people with disabilities have been competing in a wide range of sporting events. These men are taking part in the London marathon.*

Below *The Tower of London provides the scenery along one part of the course of the London marathon.*

Mass participation

The marathon is the longest running race in the Olympics programme. It is set over a distance of 42.29 km. This distance was established at the 1908 Games in London for the sole reason that the organizers wanted the race to finish in front of the royal box.

The marathons have become very popular in recent years for runners of all ages and standards. 'City' marathons take place in several countries and thousands of people take part. The New York and London marathons are 'fun runs'.

Though the runners need to train before the event takes place, few hope to win, the main purpose being to complete the course if possible, and to raise money for charity.

In March 1982, an event took place in Auckland, New Zealand that attracted a field of about 80,000 runners. This was the *Round the Bays* run over a course of 10.5 km. Events like these will probably become even more popular in the 1990s. They encourage people of all ages to enjoy sport in the company of others. They also provide good opportunities for fund-raising on a massive scale and for giving entertainment to a large number of people in the process.

Glossary

Amateur Someone who plays a sport for enjoyment and does not receive payment for doing so.

Apartheid This literally means 'apartness'. It is the official South African government policy of the separation of people of different races; that is, whites, blacks, Asians and coloureds.

Bookmaker A person who takes bets on the result of a sporting event such as a horserace or a greyhound race. Bookmakers are usually called bookies for short.

Exhibition match A match between professionals which is played before an audience to show off the skills of the players. The result of the match is not important.

Freestyle In swimming, a race in which any kind of stroke may be used.

Grand Prix races In motor racing, the races which form the basis of the racing drivers' world championship. The French words 'Grand Prix' mean great prize.

Home run In baseball, a hit which allows the striker to run a complete circuit of the bases.

International matches Games played between a number of different countries.

Leg stump In cricket, the wicket consists of three stumps. The leg stump is to the left of a right-handed batsman as he faces the bowler.

Marathon The longest regular athletics race, run over a distance of 42.29 km. This distance was established at the 1908 Olympic Games. The race was started on the lawns of Windsor Castle and finished at the stadium in Shepherd's Bush, London.

Marquis of Queensberry Rules The code of fair play in boxing that was drawn up in 1867 by the Marquis of Queensberry.

MCC Marylebone Cricket Club, owner of Lord's Cricket Ground in London, founded in 1787.

Pentathlon An athletic contest in which the competitors each take part in five events.

Professional Someone who makes a career of a particular sport and receives payment for it.

Sponsor A company or individual who pays money to a player or sporting organization in return for publicity or advertisement.

Stadium A very large sportsground, sometimes with a roof, where sporting events can take place.

Swastika The symbol used by the German Nazi Party in the 1930s and during the Second World War.

Touchdown In American football, a scoring play in which the ball is moved across the opponent's goal line.

Tour de France A cycle race throughout France, held each year. Riders have to cover over 4,000 km during a three-week period.

Tournament A series of matches to determine a winner or a winning team, by a process of elimination.

Triathlon A sporting contest in which competitors take part in three events.

Further Reading

Coe, Sebastian, and Mason, Nicholas, **The Olympians** (Pavilion, 1988).
Evans, Philip, **The World Cup** (Coronet, 1986).
Green, Robert, **Golf: An Illustrated History of the Game** (Collins, 1987).
Hammond, Tim, **Eyewitness Sport** (Dorling Kindersley, 1988).
Killanin, Lord, and Rodda, John, **The Olympic Games** (Collins, 1983).
Kilner, Simon, **Puffin Book of American Football** (Puffin, 1988).
Matthews, Peter, and Morrison, Ian, **Guinness Encyclopedia of Sports Records and Results** (Guinness, 1987).
Odd, Gilbert, **Kings of the Ring: 100 Years of Heavyweight Boxing** (Newnes, 1985).
Pinder, Steve, and Steen, Rob, **Sportswatching** (Puffin, 1988).
Swanton, E.W. (Editor), **Barclay's World of Cricket** (Collins, 1986).
Woods, Paula, **Athletics** (Usborne, 1988).

Picture Acknowledgements

The illustrations in this book were supplied by: Allsport, *front and back covers, frontispiece*, 17 (bottom), 20 (bottom), 23 (bottom), 24 (top), 25 (top), 30, 31 (bottom), 34, 35, 37, 38, 39, 41, 42 (bottom), 45; Bridgeman Art Library 4 (top), 6; Coloursport 31 (top), 32, 36, 40; E.T. Archive 4 (bottom), 10, 17; Mary Evans 5 (top), 7, 8 (top), 9, 20 (top); Hulton Picture Library 5 (bottom), 8 (bottom), 11, 12 (top), 12 (bottom right), 13, 14, 15, 16, 18, 19 (top), 22; Phil Holden 42 (top), 43; Hutchison Library 44; Macdonald / Aldus Archive 12 (bottom left), 19 (bottom), 21; Popperfoto 29 (bottom); Sporting Pictures 44; Syndication International 24 (bottom), 25 (bottom), 26; Topham Picture Library 23 (top), 28, 29.

Index

Ali, Muhammad 26
Amateurism 7, 26–7
American football, 5, 6, 23, 25, 28, 37, 40
Apartheid 30–31
Athletics 12, 23, 24

Badminton 37
Bannister, Roger 24
Baseball 5, 13, 25
Basketball 5, 8
Betting 7
Bikila, Abebe 23
Billiards 36
Black athletes 9, 21, 23, 30–31
Boxing 9, 26
  heroes 18–19, 24
  Jeffries, Jim 9
  Johnson, Jack 9
Bradman, Donald 13, 16
Budd, Zola 31

Campbell, Donald 24
Carnera, Primo 18–19
Chichester, Sir Francis 25
Cooper, Henry 26
Cousins, Robin 37
Cricket 4–5, 8
  bodyline bowling 16–17
  clothing 6
  heroes 13
  Lord's Cricket Ground 4
  professionalism 7, 27, 35
  records 13, 24
  test matches 4–5, 13, 16–17, 22, 28
  World Series 35
Cycling 28

Darts 36
Dempsey, Jack 12
Didrikson, Mildred 'Babe' 15

Ederle, Gertrude 14

Edward VII, King 7

Football (soccer) 4
  clothing 6
  Corinthians, the 8
  heroes 13
  international matches 8, 11, 17, 21, 22–3
  professionalism 7
  violence 40
  World Cup 11, 23

Golf 7, 10, 13, 15, 27, 39
Greyhound racing 17
Gymnastics 37

Hang-gliding 42
Henie, Sonja 15
Hockey 4
Horse-racing 7, 19

Ice hockey 10

Johnson, Jack 9
Jones, Bobby 12

Korbut, Olga 37

Larwood, Harold 16, 17
Laver, Rod 26, 28
Louis, Joe 19

Maradona, Diego 34,
Marathons 5, 44, 46
Moody, Helen Wills 14
Motor-racing 27, 28, 36

Netball 5
Nicklaus, Jack 34

Olympic Games 5, 10, 20–21, 27, 28, 30, 32, 43, 44
  Amsterdam 15
  Berlin 20–1, 28

Los Angeles 15, 33
Mexico City 24, 32–3
Montreal 33
Moscow 33
Munich 20–21, 33
Rome 28
Tokyo 28
Owens, Jesse 21

Packer, Kerry 35
Palmer, Arnold 27
Pelé 22
Politics 30–3
Prost, Alain 39

Rugby Union 22, 27, 28, 31
Ruth, Babe 13

Skating 10, 15
Skiing 10
Snooker 36
Sobers, Gary 24, 25
Sponsorship 38–9
Squash 37
Swimming 12, 14–15

Television 28, 36–7
Tennis 4, 5, 8
  Davis Cup 5, 30
  heroes 10
  national championships 5, 10
  professionalism 26
  records 12
  Wimbledon 10, 14, 28
  women players 10, 14
Thorpe, Jim 5
Triathlon 37, 46

Violence 40
Volleyball 5

Weissmuller, Johnny 12
Windsurfing 43
Women athletes 14–15, 37

48